W9-CAY-229

Bridgestone
BOOKS

World of Mammals

Gorillas

by Scott R. Welvaert

Consultant:
Jane T. R. Dewar
Founder
Gorilla Haven
Morganton, Georgia

Capstone
press

Mankato, Minnesota

Bridgestone Books are published by Capstone Press,
151 Good Counsel Drive, P.O. Box 669, Mankato, Minnesota 56002.
www.capstonepress.com

Library of Congress Cataloging-in-Publication Data
Welvaert, Scott R.
   Gorillas / by Scott R. Welvaert.
     p. cm.—(Bridgestone books. World of mammals)
   Includes bibliographical references and index.
   ISBN 0-7368-3718-3 (hardcover)
   1. Gorilla—Juvenile literature. I. Title. II. Series: World of Mammals.
QL737.P96W378 2005
599.884—dc22   2004013426

Summary: A brief introduction to gorillas, discussing their characteristics, habitat, life cycle, and
   predators. Includes a range map, life cycle illustration, and amazing facts.

Editorial Credits
Erika L. Shores, editor; Molly Nei, set designer; Ted Williams, book designer; Bob Lentz, illustrator;
   Kelly Garvin, photo researcher; Scott Thoms, photo editor

Photo Credits
Corbis/Gallo Images, 4, 18; Martin Harvey/Gallo Images, 10; Tom Brakefield, 16
Digital Vision/Gerry Ellis & Karl Ammann, 1
McDonald Wildlife/Mary Ann McDonald, cover
Minden Pictures/Konrad Wothe, 12
Nature Picture Library/Bruce Davidson, 6, 20

1 2 3 4 5 6 10 09 08 07 06 05

Table of Contents

Gorillas

Africa's **rain forests** are home to gentle animals called gorillas. These animals have faces, ears, and fingers like people. Gorillas also have large brains and no tails.

Gorillas and people are **primates.** Chimpanzees and monkeys are also primates. Primates are **mammals**. All mammals are **warm-blooded** and have backbones. Female mammals feed milk to their young.

◄ Each gorilla's nose is different, like a fingerprint. People can tell gorillas apart by their noses.

What Gorillas Look Like

Gorillas are big and strong. They have long arms and short legs. Adult gorillas stand about 4 to 6 feet (1.25 to 1.75 meters) tall. They weigh up to 500 pounds (230 kilograms).

Gorillas have black or brown-gray hair. Silver hair grows on the backs of older males. These males are called silverbacks. Hair usually does not grow on gorillas' faces, chests, and palms.

◄ Gorillas walk on their hands and feet. They curl up their fingers to walk on their knuckles.

Gorillas Range Map

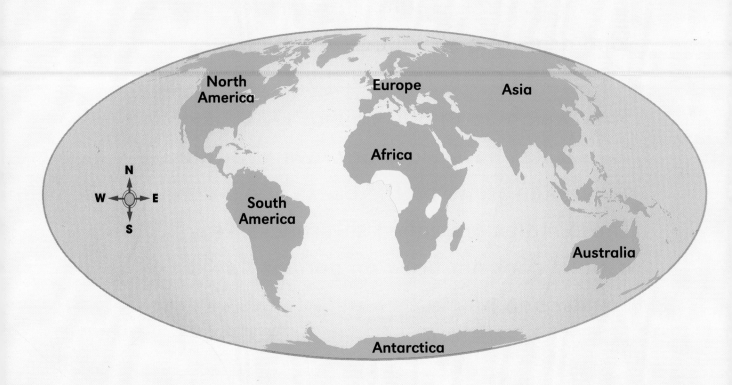

North America

Europe

Asia

Africa

South America

N
W · E
S

Australia

Antarctica

Where Gorillas Live

Gorillas in the World

Gorillas live in central Africa. Lowland gorillas live only in lowland rain forests. Lowland gorillas live in the countries of Nigeria, Cameroon, Democratic Republic of the Congo, Central African Republic, Gabon, Congo, and Equatorial Guinea.

Mountain gorillas live in rain forests in the mountains. Mountain gorillas live in Rwanda, Democratic Republic of the Congo, and Uganda.

◄ Gorillas live in parts of central Africa.

Gorilla Habitats

The rain forest **habitat** has what gorillas need to survive. Gorillas use rain forest trees and plants for shelter and food.

Gorillas make nests out of leaves and branches. Some gorillas make their nests on the forest floor. Others make their nests in trees. Gorillas make a new nest to sleep in each night.

◄ Mountain gorillas rest in leaves and grasses during the day.

What Gorillas Eat

Gorillas live near their food. Rain forest lowlands are home to many fruit trees. Gorillas there eat guavas, papayas, and other fruits from these trees. Mountain gorillas eat leaves and herbs. They also eat bamboo and wild celery. Gorillas eat up to 66 pounds (30 kilograms) of food each day.

◄ Gorillas spend most of their day looking for food.

The Life Cycle of a Gorilla

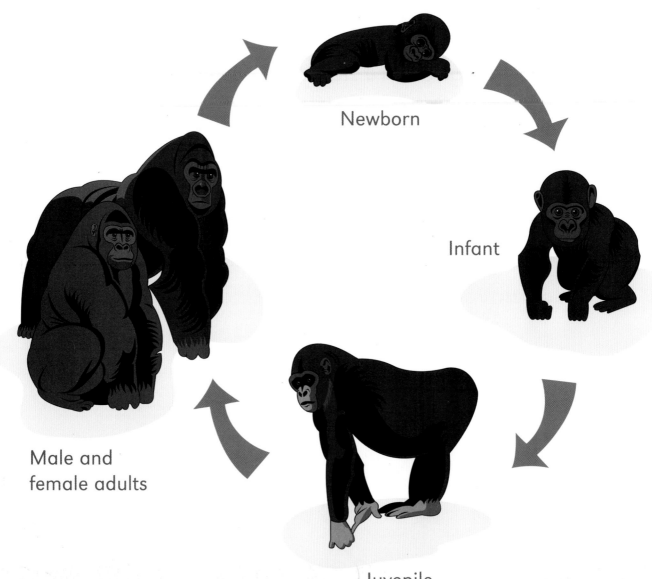

Newborn

Infant

Juvenile

Male and
female adults

14

Producing Young

Most gorillas live together in groups of three to 30 gorillas. Each group has a **dominant** silverback. This older male gorilla is the group leader.

Female gorillas **mate** with the dominant silverback to have offspring. A female gorilla gives birth to a newborn gorilla about eight months later. Female gorillas usually have only one newborn at a time. But gorillas can have twins.

Growing Up

Newborn gorillas are small. They weigh about 4 to 5 pounds (2 to 3 kilograms). Gorillas grow as they drink their mother's milk.

Infant gorillas cling to their mother for the first six months. As they grow older, young gorillas climb trees and play. Young gorillas stay with their mothers until they are 3 to 4 years old. Then they are ready to find food on their own.

◀ After four months, a gorilla infant can ride on its mother's back.

18

Dangers to Gorillas

People are the only danger to gorillas. Some people destroy gorilla habitats. They cut down rain forest trees to make farms. Some of the trees are cut down for firewood.

Poachers kill many gorillas each year. They kill gorillas for their meat. Other poachers kill adult gorillas to steal their young. The poachers sell the young gorillas to bad zoos or as pets.

Some people work to help gorillas. They want to see gorillas continue to live in Africa's rain forests.

◄ When poachers kill adult gorillas, their young cannot survive. Wildlife groups often rescue the young gorillas.

Amazing Facts about Gorillas

- Gorillas can smile, purr, and laugh. They also can cry. But gorillas cry with sounds, not with tears.

- Gorillas usually do not drink water. The food they eat gives them the water they need.

- Gorillas' big toes are just like their thumbs. They can grab things with their feet, just like with their hands.

◄ Gorillas are gentle animals. They do not attack other animals.

Glossary

dominant (DOM-uh-nuhnt)—most powerful

habitat (HAB-uh-tat)—the place and natural conditions in which an animal lives

mammal (MAM-uhl)—a warm-blooded animal that has a backbone; female mammals feed milk to their young.

mate (MAYT)—to join together to produce young

poacher (POHCH-ur)—a person who hunts certain animals even though it is against the law

primate (PRY-mate)—any animal in a group that includes humans, apes, and monkeys; primates use their four fingers and one thumb to hold objects.

rain forest (RAYN FOR-ist)—a thick area of trees where rain falls nearly every day

warm-blooded (warm-BLUHD-id)—having a body temperature that stays the same

Read More

Brend, Stephen. *Gorilla: Habitats, Life Cycles, Food Chains, Threats.* Natural World. Austin, Texas: Raintree Steck-Vaughn, 2003.

Jacobs, Liza. *Gorillas.* Wild Wild World. San Diego: Blackbirch Press, 2003.

Internet Sites

FactHound offers a safe, fun way to find Internet sites related to this book. All of the sites on FactHound have been researched by our staff.

Here's how:
1. Visit *www.facthound.com*
2. Type in this special code **0736837183** for age-appropriate sites. Or enter a search word related to this book for a more general search.
3. Click on the **Fetch It** button.

FactHound will fetch the best sites for you!

Index